W9-CUL-074

THE ROBOTICS CLUB
Teaming Up to Build Robots

THERESE SHEA

rosen publishing's
rosen
central

NEW YORK

For Mark Alexander

Published in 2011 by The Rosen Publishing Group, Inc.
29 East 21st Street, New York, NY 10010

Copyright © 2011 by The Rosen Publishing Group, Inc.

First Edition

Library of Congress Cataloging-in-Publication Data

Shea, Therese.
The robotics club: teaming up to build robots / Therese Shea. – 1st ed.
 p. cm. — (Robotics)
Includes bibliographical references and index.
ISBN 978-1-4488-1237-0 (library binding)
ISBN 978-1-4488-2251-5 (pbk.)
ISBN 978-1-4488-2256-0 (6-pack)
1. Robots–Design and construction—Juvenile literature. 2. Robotics—Juvenile literature. 3. Teenagers—Societies and clubs—Juvenile literature.
I. Title.
TJ211.2.S538 2011
629.8'92–dc22

2010025750

Manufactured in the United States of America

CPSIA Compliance Information: Batch #W11YA: For further information, contact Rosen Publishing, New York, New York, at 1-800-237-9932.

On the cover: Team 341—"Miss Daisy"—is a FIRST robotics team from Wissahickon High School in Ambler, Pennsylvania.

CONTENTS

INTRODUCTION

Years ago, robots were seen only in the pages of comic books and in movies. However, advances in computers and electronics have made robots a part of daily life. Today, perhaps only the most complex robots are even thought of as robots. In fact, sometimes it is hard to actually identify a robot. Many people still think of robots as machines with two legs that resemble people, but robots can look very different from humans.

One of the most commonly accepted definitions of "robot" is a machine that is designed to perform actions normally carried out by people or living creatures. According to this description, a robot does not need to look like a person. However, it completes tasks like a person or animal, often repeating them until programmed to do something different.

Today, robots are a reality. They paint cars in factories. They vacuum people's homes and offices. They are sometimes found in hospitals as stand-ins for doctors. Some people even have robot dogs and fish as pets. Even though they are very much a part of modern life, robots still capture people's imaginations. How much more will robots be able to do in the future?

Perhaps the best part of robots' accessibility is that the technology to build them is becoming widely available to everyone. Also, the materials needed to construct a robot are more affordable now than ever before. The interest in robotics, or the science and technology of robots, has led to the formation of robotics clubs all over the world. Robotics clubs are great ways to learn about robots, assemble them, and participate in robotics competitions. They are also an ideal setting to practice a hobby, make friends, and just have fun. Robotics clubs are helping launch the careers of young scientists every day.

Robotics clubs welcome questions and new members, as the Beach Cities Robotics Club does during its annual open house celebration.

CHAPTER 1
Building Robots

Modern robots have some basic parts. Although they can look very different, they all share common characteristics. The process of a robot's parts working together is much like the human brain working with body systems to move and act. Autonomous robots make decisions and act based on their environment.

A robot has one or more computers that act as its brain. In smaller robots, the computer is often in the form of a microcontroller, which can do even more than a microprocessor. It acts as the machine's "control," storing programs, receiving information, and sending instructions through an electrical circuit.

The circuit connects to the robot's motors (or actuators). Some robots use electric motors and electromagnets (or solenoids). Others use a hydraulic system (or pressurized fluid system) or a pneumatic system (or pressurized gas system). A robot may contain different systems, too.

The motors need power to drive them. Most robots are battery powered or plug into an electrical outlet. Hydraulic robots need a pump to pressurize the hydraulic fluid, and pneumatic robots need an air compressor or compressed air tanks.

Like a human body, a robot must have parts that move. Some robots are just wheels, while others have movable metal or plastic segments. Like bones, the segments are connected with joints. The motors are the muscles that cause the segments to move when instructed by the computer and supplied with power.

Another important feature of a robot sets it apart from a regular computer. It has the ability to react to its environment. Sensors collect environmental information and send it to the computer. Sensors collect information about movement, temperature, smell, touch, sound, and light: all things that tell people how to react. Sensors may be in the form of video cameras or temperature gauges.

ROBOTICS SAFETY

When working with robotics, as with any project involving electricity and construction tools, certain safety precautions should always be taken. Cutting corners can lead to accidents. Following some simple rules will ensure that constructing remains safe and fun.

These teammates do a last check of their team's final product before sending the robot into the 2010 FIRST Tech Challenge Championship.

FRANKENSTEIN AND THE FEAR OF ROBOTS

IN THE 1700S, THE INDUSTRIAL REVOLUTION TRANSFORMED ENGLAND. FOR THE FIRST TIME, MACHINES WERE TAKING THE PLACE OF PEOPLE IN FACTORIES. SOME WORKERS EVEN BROKE FACTORY EQUIPMENT BECAUSE THEY WERE FEARFUL OF LOSING THEIR JOBS. DURING THIS TIME OF UNCERTAINTY, MARY SHELLEY WROTE *FRANKENSTEIN*. SHELLY'S BOOK WAS ARGUABLY THE FIRST SCIENCE FICTION NOVEL—AND A HORROR STORY. THE STORY FOCUSES ON VICTOR FRANKENSTEIN, A DOCTOR AND SCIENTIST WHO BUILDS A CREATURE CALLED THE "MONSTER." THE EXPERIMENT GOES HORRIBLY WRONG. *FRANKENSTEIN* MIRRORED SOME PEOPLE'S FEAR OF TECHNOLOGY DURING THE INDUSTRIAL REVOLUTION—AND WHAT TECHNOLOGY COULD POSSIBLY CREATE CREATE.

HOWEVER, THE MORE PEOPLE EDUCATED THEMSELVES ABOUT ROBOTICS, THE MORE THEY ACKNOWLEDGED THE POSITIVE EFFECTS OF THE TECHNOLOGY. GEORGE DEVOL AND JOSEPH ENGELBERGER BUILT WHAT MANY CONSIDER TO BE THE FIRST MODERN ROBOT, WHICH THEY CALLED UNIMATE. IT POSSESSED SENSORS AND PERFORMED TASKS LIKE A HUMAN ARM—A 4,000-POUND (1,814-KILOGRAM) ARM. UNIMATE GOT ITS FIRST JOB IN 1961 STACKING HOT METAL ON A CAR ASSEMBLY LINE.

- Check with an adult before beginning a project.

- Read directions closely before starting work.

- Work in a well-lit environment.

- Use robots only for the tasks they are meant to perform. They should not handle dangerous materials.

- Robots may move without warning when connected with their power source.

- Wear eye protection when working on or operating robots.

ROBOT KITS AND PARTS

A robot is as complex as its builder wants it to be. Robot-building competitions include people as young as six years old. This shows what an accessible hobby robotics has become.

Some roboticists buy kits, such as LEGO Mindstorms or kits that robot shops put together, that include nearly all the materials they need to build a robot. Common household tools such as screwdrivers and pliers may be needed as well. Kit materials can usually be used again and again.

Others enjoy picking out their own robot parts. Supplies can be found at hobby shops and online robotics suppliers. This way, they can select bigger wheels, more powerful motors, or any other things they need for their creation. A quick Internet search can show beginners the different kinds of robots they can make. However, even the simplest machines have wheels (or other movable parts), motors, rechargeable batteries, a microcontroller, and sensors. Microcontrollers and sensors come with detailed explanations of how to use and program them.

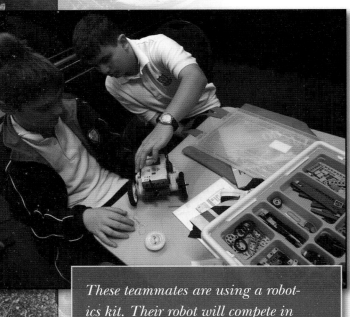

These teammates are using a robotics kit. Their robot will compete in dance, soccer, and rescue events in the RoboCupJunior competition.

Robotics materials can be expensive, which makes robotics clubs even more useful for roboticists. In addition to sharing knowledge and enthusiasm, people can pool robotics parts and resources. Although robotics is not a free pastime, it is an investment in the future—future robots, fun, and friends.

CHAPTER 2
Starting a Robotics Club

When people are enthusiastic about a rock band or a movie star, they join a fan club. When they are enthusiastic about robots, they join a robotics club. All kinds of people join robotics clubs: beginners who have never built a robot, experts who can share their knowledge, fans who want entertainment, builders who want to put their robots in competitions, and people hoping to make new friends.

Robotics clubs can be found all over the world. There are community robotics clubs, school robotics clubs, and online robotics clubs. People of all ages join these clubs, though some are meant for certain age groups. However, many communities and schools do not have

The Magruder High School robotics club, together with mentors from the U.S. Commerce Department, designed and built a robot that can stack inflated tubes.

robotics clubs. Here are some tips for forming a robotics club if there isn't one near you.

WHERE AND WHEN TO MEET

First, a robotics club needs a place to meet. It should be somewhere with enough room for an expanding club. A member's bedroom is probably not sufficient. However, the space does not have to accommodate people building their robots. Often, robotics club meetings are for discussions. The building takes place at home, or special meetings are arranged for people to work on their projects together. Some meeting space ideas are school classrooms, library meeting rooms, coffee shops, or someone's living room or garage. All of these places require permission to use the area as a meeting space. Let an adult or supervisor know how many people are expected and what materials are needed, such as chairs and tables.

A regular meeting time should be established—perhaps once a month on a certain day. For example, a meeting could take place every third Tuesday of the month at 7 o'clock. This way, people know in advance when the meeting will be and can make plans to attend. Special dates can be set up for workshops or guest speakers if needed.

GETTING PEOPLE TO JOIN

So the club has a place and a time to meet. How does it get people to show up? Luckily, there are many ways to spread the word. An old-fashioned but effective method is word of mouth. If a club member tells a friend or classmate, that person will tell other people. If each member tells two or three people, word will

A Web site, such as www.team341.com, can give practical information and show a team's personality and creativity.

really get around. Another way to let people know is by e-mail.

There are robotics club Web sites where anyone can post information about their robotics group. Posting on a robotics site is helpful because the users are already interested in robotics. There may be similar robotics pages on social networking Web sites. Make sure to ask an adult about posting information on the Internet. A danger of communicating openly online is that anyone can read about the club. In fact, it is a good idea if an adult is always present at club meetings.

After the club starts, it is also possible to create a Web site or start an online discussion group. Information can be posted about meetings, allowing people to chat about what happened at the meeting and providing a place for members to chat about their current robotics projects. It could be a helpful troubleshooting site for those building robots as well.

CLUB POSITIONS

In many clubs, various roles must be filled to help shoulder the many responsibilities. The president of the club represents the club to the outside world. He or she promises that the club will operate to best serve the needs of the members. A secretary arranges for events and records information at meetings. A treasurer is responsible for collecting and dispensing money. When a club is first starting out, it may not need these positions. However, the larger it gets, the more responsibility will need to be shared. This way, chores and tasks are shouldered by all members, and everyone has time to construct and tinker with robotics.

RUNNING A MEETING

What happens when people show up at a robotics club meeting? There should be a plan of action, or an agenda, so that the meeting runs smoothly. Many clubs print out agendas so that members know the plans and discussion topics for the club that day. It may also be wise to assign a certain amount of time to each part of the agenda. An agenda for a one-hour meeting might look like this:

A. *Introductions (five minutes)*
B. *Previous discussions/previous business (ten minutes)*
C. *Presentations/lectures by a group member or a special guest (fifteen minutes)*
D. *Announcements of competitions and upcoming events (five minutes)*
E. *Show-and-tell/sharing of information (twenty minutes)*
F. *Ideas for next meeting (five minutes)*

INTRODUCTIONS

Introductions are essential when the group meets for the first time. People need to get to know each other and feel that the club is a friendly environment. For the first few meetings, it would be a good idea for club members to wear name tags. After a while, people won't need name tags. However, it is always a good idea to introduce new people to the club. Perhaps one person can be in charge of "hospitality"—making people feel welcome in the club.

PREVIOUS DISCUSSIONS/PREVIOUS BUSINESS

Since a club meeting lasts for only a certain amount of time, sometimes topics are not fully discussed or need to be put on hold until the next meeting. Perhaps not everyone's ideas were heard. Some time should be set aside to finish up old business before new discussions. For example, imagine a club discussion focuses on a field trip the members would like to take. After the meeting, a member may hear about a new robotics museum that is opening. In the next meeting, during the "old discussions" part of the meeting, the member would have time to mention the museum.

PRESENTATIONS/LECTURES BY A GROUP MEMBER OR A SPECIAL GUEST

Part of the reason many people join robotics clubs is to learn. A valuable part of any meeting is instruction time. A presentation by a club member could help someone understand aspects of his or her own projects and robots. In fact, one of the first meetings could be a presentation on how to make a simple robot.

This time in the meeting might also be used to have a special guest talk to the group. Someone who has a career in robotics can explain the preparation necessary for a similar career path.

ANNOUNCEMENTS OF COMPETITIONS AND UPCOMING EVENTS

After people have learned about and built their own robots, they will want to show them to others. Robotics competitions are a great showroom. This time in the club's agenda can focus on upcoming competitions so that club members can decide if they have what it takes to enter. They might also want to go as spectators. Be sure to list all event details, such as time, place, entrance fees, and transportation details.

ROBOT DOCTORS

MANY PEOPLE THINK OF ROBOTICS AS A SINGLE FIELD OF STUDY. HOWEVER, ROBOTICS WILL HAVE AN IMPACT ON ALL CAREERS IN THE FUTURE. FOR EXAMPLE, MICROBOTS HAVE FAR-REACHING IMPLICATIONS FOR MEDICINE. THESE TINY ROBOTS ARE CURRENTLY ABOUT .80-INCH (2-CENTIMETERS) LONG. HOWEVER, SCIENTISTS HOPE TO CREATE ROBOTS, CALLED NANOROBOTS, IN THE NEAR FUTURE THAT ARE MUCH, MUCH SMALLER. THEY WILL BE MOSTLY AUTONO-MOUS MACHINES, WHICH WILL BE SENT INTO THE HUMAN BODY TO COMBAT AILMENTS SUCH AS HEART DISEASE AND CANCER.

As the robotics club grows, it may also want to hold its own competitions. First, the members can compete against each other. Then, they can challenge other clubs. If the robotics club holds a competition, there are many details to discuss, such as the kind of competition, who will judge, where it will be held, and what the prizes will be.

SHOW-AND-TELL/SHARING OF INFORMATION

Most people join robotics clubs to see robots and show off their own. For the last part of each meeting, have a show-and-tell. Each club member can demonstrate and explain his or her progress on a project. After everyone is done, people can ask each other questions about their work and share information.

Some people who join the club will want to attend a few meetings before starting their own robot. Beginners may be frustrated or intimidated to show their simpler robots to people who have been building for years. Perhaps newbies can get together outside club meetings to start a project together.

Put some time aside during the meeting to see if anyone has anything more they would like to share with the group. They might have a tip about a robotics equipment sale or a new Web site to check out.

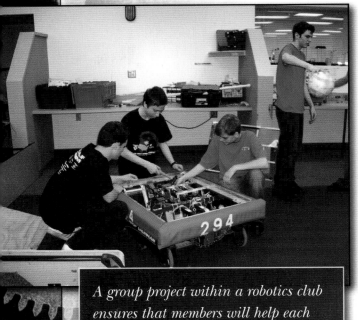

A group project within a robotics club ensures that members will help each other learn and share new ideas.

IDEAS FOR THE NEXT MEETING

Before the meeting ends, remind everyone of the next meeting date. Mention what will happen at the next meeting, such as a presentation by a guest speaker. If nothing is scheduled, ask for ideas from the members regarding new topics to cover. If meetings are run well and are helpful to builders, members will be excited to keep coming back.

CLUB RESPONSIBILITIES

After a few meetings, members need to decide whether to collect dues for the club. Dues are money that helps an organization in various ways. For example, if the club meetings include pizza and soda for members each month, each club member may want to pay a few dollars in dues so one person doesn't have to buy the food and drink for everyone else each month. If the club wants to invest in special tools or equipment to share, these expenses could be covered under club dues as well. Don't forget the trophies for club competitions.

MENTORS

The most successful robotics clubs also work with mentors. It's handy to have an expert around. Robotics mentors are often engineers who volunteer to advise, teach, and encourage club members to achieve their potential. There will be times when a project seems too difficult or confusing to complete. Mentors guide the club in developing their own solution rather than telling them what to do. Many engineering companies provide mentors for robotics clubs.

SPONSORS

Some robotics club activities can be quite expensive. When member dues are not enough, it may become necessary to find club sponsors. These are companies that give monetary aid to clubs to help them buy equipment or enter competitions that require large fees. In exchange for the help, some teams wear shirts with their sponsors' names or logos or offer thanks (and free advertising) on their club Web sites. Sponsors may be companies related to the robotics field or local businesses interested in investing in future roboticists.

CHAPTER 3
Competitions

Once the members of a robotics club complete their first robots, the time has come to see what the machines can do and how they measure up to other robots. Not only do robot competitions give roboticists a chance to show off, but they are learning opportunities. Participants acquire knowledge of how to improve their robots and their robots' performances.

There are a few basic kinds of robotics competitions. Some may be appropriate to hold within a club meeting. Others require many competing robots, so other robotics clubs should be invited to participate. An important consideration is that many major competitions require that robots are autonomous. Remote controls are often not allowed. The builder must let their robot's programming, motors, and sensors do their jobs. A well-constructed robot can move through an environment and react based on information obtained by its sensors.

BASIC TABLETOP

A tabletop competition is ideal for beginners. It requires a robot to travel to different areas on a field. Think of a football player running from one end zone to the other and back. Since the contest most likely takes place on a table, one part of the challenge is to make a robot that will stop without falling off one end. Each robot gets a number of chances to complete the course. There are certain time limits for each chance. If a person needs to help his or her robot, that attempt may be considered over.

Robots are usually allowed on the tabletop course one at a time. Because many robots may complete the basic requirements, the contest is often broken down into point values. For example, reaching one zone may award a contestant ten points, reaching the second zone may add another ten points, and extra points

The ILITE (Inspiring Leaders in Technology and Engineering) Robotics Team 1885 shows enthusiasm for competition at the 2010 World Championships.

may be given for speed. Sometimes, points are given out for entertainment value. If a contestant builds a robot that raises a victory flag, plays a song, or takes a bow, the crowd will love it.

BASIC LINE FOLLOWING

A basic line following competition tests a robot's ability to follow a track on a course. Robots compete for accuracy and speed. Since remote controls are not allowed, the robot must be able to follow the line using only prior programming and its sensors. In these competitions, builders decide how many sensors will help their robots "read" and complete the course in a quick and precise manner.

If a robot goes off course, a certain number of points are deducted depending on whether it can find its way back onto the course or whether its builder needs to intervene. Often, each robot is allowed three chances to complete the course. The speediest time is recorded. Courses with obstacles make line following more challenging for advanced robots.

SUMO

In a sumo wrestling competition, two large people attempt to push each other out of a circle. It takes strength, balance, and an ability to anticipate what the other person will do. Similarly, in sumo robotics competitions, two robots try to push each other outside of a circle. The first robot that touches the outside of the competition ring loses a round. The contest is the best out of three rounds.

This robot competes in an event called Breakaway, designed for a FIRST Robotics Competition. Tunnels were also part of the 2010 challenge.

There are usually restrictions on what robots can do within the sumo ring. For example, robots can't helicopter above the ring or shoot fire at opponents. There are usually weight limitations, too, so that the contest is more difficult than a heavy robot pushing a light robot out of the ring. Instead, robots "trick" their opponents by using lights that confuse sensors and magnets and suction to stay in place. Robots can also split into several parts once the contest starts. However, any robot part that travels outside the ring loses the round for the robot.

Judges set a time limit for each round. They may choose to end a round if robots don't touch or become locked together, or if a time limit passes. In the event of a tie, a judge may declare the lighter robot the winner. A judge may also make suggestions to competitors about how they can make changes to their robots for more durability in the next event.

HUMANOID ROBOT COMPETITIONS

Robotics competitions for more advanced builders may involve humanoid robots. Sometimes, the contest is as simple as a two-legged humanoid robot walking up and down stairs. However, it is not so simple to build and program a robot that can do this. Balance is a key skill and challenge.

Another kind of humanoid competition pits the robots against each other in martial arts contests. Each robot attempts to "knock out" its opponent. These kinds of contests often allow for remote control, since they are considered difficult. All robots in these competitions must walk on two legs.

FIRST

FIRST's various robotics competitions are for robot builders from kindergarten to twelfth grade. FIRST stands for "For Inspiration and Recognition of Science and Technology." In 1989, FIRST was founded by Dean Kamen, inventor of the two-wheeled electric vehicle called a Segway. This organization encourages elementary and high school students to pursue careers in science, technology, and engineering. More than $12 million in scholarships are given out as prizes.

The initial FIRST Robotics Competition (for grades nine through twelve) took place in 1992 and involved

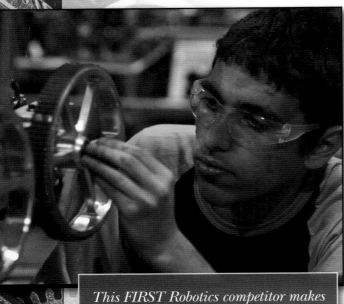

This FIRST Robotics competitor makes a last-minute adjustment before his team's robot rolls into the spotlight.

twenty-eight teams in a New Hampshire high school gym. The 2010 FIRST Robotics Competition involved 1,809 teams and 45,225 students from twelve countries. FIRST Robotics Competition (FRC) robots are built from kits provided to teams six weeks before the regional rounds prior to the main championship. They weigh up to 120 pounds (54 kg), excluding battery and bumpers. Also included in the kit is the description of the game for that year. The regional winners are invited to compete in the national championship.

The FIRST Tech Challenge (FTC) was also established for the high school age group. The robotics kits for this competition are more affordable than those for the other competition. FIRST Tech challenges are different year to year as well.

For robot builders ages nine to sixteen, FIRST has a LEGO League. More than 147,000 people from fifty-six different countries take part in this competition. Teams use LEGO Mindstorms technology to build their robots. LEGO Mindstorms kits have LEGO blocks, sensors, motors, and computer software. LEGO League competitors build according to a theme. The 2010 theme was "engineering meets medicine." Robots demonstrated ways

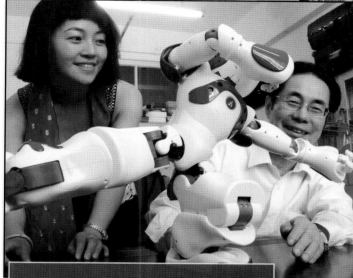

With their many joints, humanoid robots can mimic human movement. This robot shows off its ability to balance as it stands on one leg.

that science helps the body repair injuries and become better and stronger. Junior Lego Leaguers tackled the topic in a different way. These competitors are as young as six years old.

INTERNATIONAL ROBOT OLYMPIAD

Considering the amazing tasks that robots can be designed and programmed to perform, it is no surprise that there is a robot Olympics. The Robot Olympiad is an offshoot of a competition called Robot World Cup. While the World Cup is a contest for college students, the Robot Olympiad is open to students of all ages. The first Olympiad took place in 1999.

Similar to the Olympics, participating countries hold national Olympiads. The winning team from each country attends the international Olympiad. It has been staged in Korea, Malaysia, Singapore, and Australia. The competition in the past has included races similar to tabletop contests, events in which robots threw objects into baskets, robot building, race courses with ramps and obstacles, and mazes.

BOTBALL

Botball is an educational robotics program that centers on more than just building and competition. Students use science, engineering, technology, math, and writing skills in hands-on projects. The Botball year is divided into four parts that correspond with the seasons. In the fall, the Botball Research and Design Website Challenge explores a different topic in robotics each year. Students research a question, apply a solution in a design-related task, and present their work on a Web site. In the winter, workshops for teachers and team leaders explore current robotics technology and how to apply it in classrooms or communities. Information and the building materials for competing robots are then distributed for the Botball tournaments in the spring.

For Botball competitions, student teams have seven to nine weeks to build their robots for the Botball regional tournament. The robots are programmed to move around a field in a fast-paced, point-scoring game without a remote control.

In summer, students, teachers, robotics fans, and professionals from around the world gather for the annual Conference on Educational Robotics. Students and teachers exchange ideas on a range of topics. The regional champions of the Botball competitions participate in the International Botball Tournament at this conference.

ROBOCUP

Just as there is a robotic counterpart to the Olympics, there is a robotic World Cup soccer tournament. The World Cup for robots is called RoboCup. The organization behind this competition chose soccer as the main skills event because the mechanics of the sport involve many problem-solving opportunities for robot builders. The robots need to race, kick, and work together against another team. There are different leagues. Some leagues consist of small robots, and some have robots as tall as human beings.

ASIMOV AND THE RULES OF ROBOTICS

AS SCIENCE FICTION BECAME POPULAR IN THE TWENTIETH CENTURY, ROBOTS SHOWED UP IN MORE BOOKS AND IN THE PAGES OF COMIC BOOKS. ROBOTS WERE SHOWN AS EITHER EVIL OR GOOD. SCIENCE FICTION WRITER ISAAC ASIMOV TOOK THE CONCEPT OF ROBOTS AND BROUGHT THEM BACK TO SCIENCE. HE WROTE ABOUT THEM AS MACHINES AND USED THE WORD "ROBOTICS" FOR THE FIRST TIME. IN A 1942 SHORT STORY CALLED "RUNAROUND," HE LISTED THE "RULES OF ROBOTICS":

1. A ROBOT MAY NOT INJURE A HUMAN BEING, OR, THROUGH INACTION, ALLOW A HUMAN BEING TO COME TO HARM.

2. A ROBOT MUST OBEY THE ORDERS GIVEN IT BY HUMAN BEINGS EXCEPT WHERE SUCH ORDERS WOULD CON- FLICT WITH THE FIRST LAW.

3. A ROBOT MUST PROTECT ITS OWN EXISTENCE AS LONG AS SUCH PROTECTION DOES NOT CONFLICT WITH THE FIRST OR SECOND LAW.

EVEN SCIENTISTS BELIEVE THESE FAMOUS RULES ARE GOOD SAFETY MEASURES FOR THOSE CREATING AND CONTROL- LING ROBOTS. COMPETITIONS LIKE BOTBALL STRESS THAT THE ROBOTS HAVE NONDESTRUCTIVE FUNCTIONS.

OTHER EVENTS

A competition connected to RoboCup, called RoboCupRescue, focuses on constructing robots that could help with disaster rescues. In RoboCupJunior, which is for robot builders under the age of eighteen, competitors compete in similar events, as well as robot dancing.

VEX Robotics Design System, once a supplier of parts for the FIRST Tech Challenge, now sponsors the annual VEX Robotics Competition and encourages instruction of robotics within classrooms.

More competitions and tournaments than those described in this book take place each year. Even if a builder is just a beginner, knowing the requirements of competitions and seeing the kinds of robots that are constructed gives an understanding of what robotics can accomplish. Similar robots can be anyone's future goal.

The kits used to build the robots are also useful to examine. Notice that in competitions such as FIRST and Botball every team receives a similar materials kit. However, some robots emerge victorious over others. This shows how important programming, creativity, and strategy are for winning competitions. Check the back of this book for more information on these competitions and others.

CHAPTER 4
Robotics Clubs in Action

Cooperation is an important part of every robotics club. Each member has a part in transforming knowledge, inspiration, and parts into an award-winning robot.

What's more helpful than reading about how to put a robotics club together? Reading about a real robotics club in action. The robotics club of Penfield High School near Rochester, New York, is a championship competitor. Its members make up the FIRST Robotics Team 1511. They call their club Rolling Thunder. Rolling Thunder won the FIRST Championship Rookie All-Star Award in 2004—their first year of existence.

Rolling Thunder members divide responsibilities and are accountable for specific tasks. Their team exhibits knowledge, skills, creativity, and hard work in every competition. The large team is divided into the following smaller teams:

- **Leadership:** responsible for the team calendar and activities.

- **Mechanical/Construction:** designs (often with the help of a computer program) and puts together the mechanical parts of the robot.

- **Electrical:** designs and produces electrical systems for the robot.

- **Programming:** creates the code that makes the robot work. CAD (computer-aided design) is a big part of creating a successful FRC robot.

- **Finance:** responsible for fund-raising and spending.

- **Web site:** creates and maintains the Web site.

- **Strategy/Control/Rules:** controls the robot. This team is the expert on rules and creates strategies for the best scores.

- **Spirit/Logo:** creates team logos, clothing, and promotional materials.

- **Animation:** learns animation programs in preparation for animation competition.

On Rolling Thunder, there is room for future engineers and for those who just enjoy learning and being part of a team.

PREP WORK

The club does not meet only for the six weeks leading up to the regional competitions—they work year-round. Rolling Thunder members complete hundreds of hours of community service, demonstrate robotics to the community, recruit new members, find financial sponsors as well as mentors, help out other teams at competitions, and even start teams and clubs in other countries. For their efforts, this club won the Chairman's Award at the 2010 FIRST

Computer programs help robotics clubs design a robot before construction begins. Members work in small groups before pooling their ideas and work.

regional compe-
tition in Boston,
Massachusetts. The
award honors the
team that judges
believe serves
as a model to
other teams. This
very high honor
qualified Rolling
Thunder for the
2010 Championship
in Atlanta, Georgia.

Members of 2 Train Robotics, shown above, were recognized for their accomplishments by the New York Yankees in Yankee Stadium.

CHAMPIONSHIP CHALLENGE

The 2010 FIRST Robotics Competition challenge was called Breakaway. Two alliances each made up of three teams compete in a match. The goal is for one alliance to score more points than the other alliance by shooting balls into the opponent's two goals. The carpeted field is divided into three sections by bumps and tunnels. At the end of the match, alliances score extra points by lifting their robot above the platform of their alliance's tower.

The match starts with a fifteen-second autonomous period, during which robots can use programmed code and sensors to score balls into the four goals. After the

ROBOTS THAT FEEL?

CYNTHIA BREAZEAL, A ROBOTICIST SPECIALIZING IN ARTIFI-
CIAL INTELLIGENCE AT THE MASSACHUSETTS INSTITUTE OF
TECHNOLOGY, CREATED A ROBOT "BABY" CALLED KISMET.
KISMET SHOWS EMOTIONS THROUGH ITS FACIAL EXPRES-
SIONS AND MOVEMENTS. IT HAS FIFTEEN COMPUTERS TO
PROCESS INFORMATION COLLECTED BY ITS SENSORS. PEOPLE
TALK TO KISMET, AND THE ROBOT RESPONDS AS A BABY
MIGHT. AT ONE POINT, CYNTHIA THOUGHT THAT KISMET
MIGHT NEED TO BE FIXED BECAUSE IT WASN'T REACTING TO
ITS ENVIRONMENT. THE STUDENT WORKING WITH KISMET
WAS DISCOURAGED. SHE ASKED IT, "DON'T YOU LIKE ME
ANYMORE?" THEN KISMET STARTED SOOTHING HER, AS IF TO
SAY, "YES, I DO LIKE YOU. I'M SORRY."

PEOPLE ALL OVER READ ABOUT CYNTHIA BREAZEAL AND
KISMET. HOLLYWOOD DIRECTOR STEVEN SPIELBERG ASKED
HER TO HELP IN THE MAKING OF HIS MOVIE ABOUT ROBOTS,
AI: ARTIFICIAL INTELLIGENCE. CYNTHIA BELIEVES THAT IN
THE FUTURE, ROBOTS LIKE KISMET COULD BE COMPANIONS
FOR PEOPLE AND PERHAPS EVEN "GROW UP" AND LEARN
AS PEOPLE LEARN.

autonomous period, a two-minute period begins in which
team drivers take control of their robots and try to score
balls, defend goals, and keep balls on their alliance's side
of the field. In the last twenty seconds of the match, robots
are allowed to expand their size and elevate themselves.

ROBOTICS CLUBS BUILD THE FUTURE

Robotics clubs build robots that perform a variety of tasks. The question remains whether a complex robot can actually be "intelligent." How many computers and how much programming would it take to equal a human brain? Robots are being built that need less and less human intervention to complete more and more tasks.

Robotics competitions require robots to handle multiple tasks. These two robots compete to control the balls in a contest.

Many of the past members of the Rolling Thunder team graduated high school and entered college to study engineering, computer science, and other technology-related fields. Their experiences with their robotics club gave them an invaluable head start in their education and careers. Robotics clubs provide the best classroom and real-life experiences available to young roboticists today.

Interview with Team
Rolling Thunder

The best way to learn about a robotics club is to hear about its experience. Here are a few questions posed to members of Team 1511 Penfield Rolling Thunder and their answers:

What is the mission of your club?

We create opportunities for the future by providing students with robotics expertise with local engineers, and thus instill confidence to succeed in a rapidly changing world.

How many people are in your club?

Thirty-seven students and twenty-six adults/mentors.

How often do you meet?

Every Tuesday, we have a meeting from 6 to 8 PM. However, we often meet other times during the week or weekend to do fun activities, demonstrate the robot at various places, do community service projects together, etc.

Do you have requirements of your members?

We have "achievements," which are contributions like fund-raising, community service, robot demos,

AND PARENT INVOLVEMENT. STUDENTS EARN THEIR COMPE-
TITION TRIP COSTS BY COMPLETING THE ACHIEVEMENTS. (A
STUDENT WHO COMPLETES 100 PERCENT OF THE ACHIEVE-
MENTS PAYS $0 TOWARD HIS OR HER TRIPS.)

WHAT MATERIALS DO YOU USE TO BUILD ROBOTS?

ALUMINUM, WIRES, CABLES, WHEELS, NETTING/SCREENS,
LEXAN, BATTERIES, SENSORS, ROBOT CONTROLLER (CRIO)—
THESE MATERIALS DEPEND ON THAT YEAR'S OBJECTIVE AS
WE BUILD A DIFFERENT ROBOT EVERY YEAR.

WHERE DO YOU GET YOUR MATERIALS?

WE BUY FROM VARIOUS STORES, AND SOME ARE PROVIDED
BY VARIOUS SPONSORS. SOMETIMES, WE DESIGN AND MANU-
FACTURE OUR OWN CUSTOM PARTS.

HOW IMPORTANT IS COMPETITION TO YOUR CLUB?

COMPETITION IS DEFINITELY THE MOST EXCITING TIME FOR
OUR TEAM BECAUSE WE FINALLY GET TO SEE OUR HARD WORK
IN ACTION. WE ALSO GET TO MEET OTHER TEAMS, TRAVEL TO
DIFFERENT PARTS OF THE COUNTRY, AND JUST HAVE FUN.

WHAT WAS YOUR MOST SUCCESSFUL COMPETITION?

THE MOST SUCCESSFUL COMPETITION WAS OUR LAST COM-
PETITION IN BOSTON FROM MARCH 25–27, 2010. WE WERE
RANKED SECOND OUT OF FIFTY-THREE TEAMS AND MADE IT

TO THE FINALS WITH TWO SUCCESSFUL ALLIANCE PARTNERS, AND OUR ROBOT WAS WORKING WELL. WE ALSO WON THE MOST PRESTIGIOUS AWARD, THE CHAIRMAN'S AWARD, WHICH RECOGNIZES US AS BEING A ROLE MODEL TEAM FOR OTHER TEAMS. ONE OF OUR TEAM LEADERS WON A TOP AWARD, THE DEAN'S LIST, WHICH RECOGNIZES AN INDIVIDUAL STUDENT'S HARD WORK AND LEADERSHIP. JUST TWO STUDENTS ARE SELECTED TO WIN THIS AWARD AT EACH REGIONAL COMPETITION.

WHAT IS THE BEST PART OF THE CLUB?

WE'RE A FAMILY. — LEANNE B., STUDENT

EVERYONE CONTRIBUTES AND HELPS OUT WITH THINGS ON THE TEAM. IF SOMEONE IS UNABLE TO DO SOMETHING FOR SOME REASON, THE REST OF THE TEAM COMES TOGETHER TO GET IT DONE. THIS IS REALLY A SPECIAL ATTRIBUTE TO OUR TEAM AND SOMETHING WE SHOULD BE PROUD OF. — LARRY L., STUDENT

NO MATTER WHAT MATURITY LEVEL A STUDENT HAS WHEN THEY JOIN, THEY ALL GRADUATE HIGH SCHOOL AS A WELL-ROUNDED AND CONFIDENT LEADER (WITH THE COURAGE TO TAKE RISKS). — BECCA H., STUDENT

YOU GET TO MEET A LOT OF PEOPLE WITH THE SAME INTERESTS AS YOUR OWN AND MAKE FRIENDS WITH ALL OF THEM. WHEN I FIRST JOINED ROBOTICS, I WAS THE KID THAT SAT IN THE BACK CORNER OF THE CAFETERIA AND DIDN'T SAY MUCH. AFTER THE FIRST MEETING, PEOPLE WOULDN'T LET ME SIT IN THE BACK ANYMORE AND DRAGGED ME TOWARDS

THE GROUP. AFTER THAT, I MADE FRIENDS WITH A LOT OF PEOPLE AND NEVER SAT IN THE BACK AGAIN. — RIKA L., GRADUATED STUDENT

AS A MENTOR, THE BEST PART IS GETTING TO SEE THE STUDENTS COME IN AS SHY KIDS, OFTEN UNSURE OF THEIR DIRECTION OR TRUE PLACE, AND GROW INTO CONFIDENT LEADERS WHO ARE EXCITED ABOUT SCIENCE AND TECHNOLOGY AND HAVE FOUND A PLACE, A FAMILY, WHERE THEY TRULY "FIT IN." GETTING THE CHANCE TO INTERACT WITH THESE STUDENTS, AND PUSH THEM BEYOND THEIR COMFORT ZONES, HELPING THEM RISE TO THEIR POTENTIALS AND LEARN TO NOT BE AFRAID TO FAIL. IT'S A PLACE WHERE EXCITEMENT ABOUT SCIENCE AND TECHNOLOGY BRINGS TOGETHER A TRUE FAMILY. — KIM, MENTOR

THE SENSE OF ACCOMPLISHMENT YOU GET WHEN YOU REALIZE YOU JUST WENT FROM SCRATCH TO A ROBOT IS HUGE.

CALVIN D., STUDENT

GLOSSARY

artificial intelligence A branch of computer science devoted to the development of computer programs that allow machines to perform functions normally requiring human intelligence.

humanoid A being from another planet that has the appearance or characteristics of a human.

mentor One who is usually older or more experienced, who provides advice and support.

microcontroller A chip that contains a central processing unit, memory for a program, memory for input and output information, a clock, and a control unit.

microprocessor The central processing unit that performs basic operations in a computer. It consists of an integrated circuit contained on a single chip.

program To insert coded operating instructions into a machine.

promotional Material created by an organization so that people will become aware of the organization.

recruit To enroll someone as a worker or member.

roboticist One who designs, builds, programs, and experiments with robots.

sensor A device capable of detecting and responding to physical environmental factors, such as movement, light, or heat.

software Computer programs and applications.

sponsor Providing money to a charitable cause or group for an organized event.

vacuum tube A glass tube surrounding an area from which all gases have been removed. When electricity is applied to it, a current flows through the vacuum.

FOR MORE INFORMATION

Association of Computer Machinery (ACM)
2 Penn Plaza, Suite 701
New York, NY 10121-0701
(800) 342-6626
Web site: http://www.acm.org
The ACM runs special-interest groups that work on specific areas of computer science, including robotics. The organization offers online books and courses for members. It accepts student members.

Computer History Museum
1401 North Shoreline Boulevard
Mountain View, CA 94043
(650) 810-1010
Web site: http://www.computerhistory.org
In addition to on-site exhibits, the Computer History Museum maintains an illustrated history of the computer online.

FIRST Robotics Canada
Richard Yasui
FIRST Robotics Administrator
Toronto District School Board
140 Borough Drive, Level 1
Toronto, ON M1P 4N6
Canada
(416) 396-5907
Web site: http://www.firstroboticscanada.org
This organization sponsors robotics competitions for students at schools throughout Canada.

Institute of Electrical and Electronics Engineers:
Robotics and Automation Society
1828 L Street NW, Suite 1202
Washington, DC 20036-5104
(800) 678-4333
Web site: http://www.ieee-ras.org
This organization provides information for the use of
    students in computer and technology fields, includ-
    ing robotics.

The Robotics Institute
Carnegie Mellon University
5000 Forbes Avenue
Pittsburgh, PA 15213-3890
(412) 268-3818
Web site: http://www.ri.cmu.edu
This educational institution sponsors events that are
    open to the public and provides online information
    on research into robotics.

WEB SITES

Due to the changing nature of Internet links, Rosen
Publishing has developed an online list of Web sites
related to the subject of this book. This site is updated
regularly. Please use this link to access the list:

http://www.rosenlinks.com/robo/trc

FOR FURTHER READING

Angelo, Joseph A. *Robot Spacecraft*. New York, NY: Facts On File, 2006.

Asimov, Isaac. *I, Robot*. New York, NY: Spectra, 2008.

Brown, Henry T. *507 Mechanical Movements: Mechanisms and Devices*. Mineola, NY: Dover Books, 2005.

Čapek, Karel. *R.U.R.* New York, NY: Penguin Books, 2004.

Cook, David. *Robot Building for Beginners*. Berkeley, CA: Apress, 2010.

Dick, Phillip. *Do Androids Dream of Electric Sheep?* New York, NY: Oxford University Press, 2007.

Henderson, Harry. *Modern Robotics: Building Versatile Machines*. New York, NY: Chelsea House, 2007.

Ichibah, Daniel. *Robots from Science Fiction to Technological Revolution*. New York, NY: Harry Abrams, 2005.

Jefferis, David. *Robot Workers*. New York, NY: Crabtree, 2006.

Jones, David. *Mighty Robots: Mechanical Marvels That Fascinate and Frighten*. Toronto, Canada: Annick Press, 2005.

Miller, Michael. *Absolute Beginner's Guide to Computer Science*. New York, NY: Que Publishing/Pearson Technology, 2009.

National Geographic. *Robots to Motorized Monocycles*. Washington, DC: National Geographic, 2009.

Piddock, Charles. *National Geographic Investigates: Future Tech: From Personal Robots to Motorized Monocycles*. Washington, DC: National Geographic, 2009.

Whitby, Blay. *Artificial Intelligence*. New York, NY: Rosen Publishing Group, 2009.

White, Steve. *Military Robots*. Danbury, CT: Children's Press, 2007.

BIBLIOGRAPHY

BBC News. "Timeline: Real Robots." September 10, 2001. Retrieved March 30, 2010. (http://news.bbc.co.uk/2/hi/in_depth/sci_tech/2001/artificial_intelligence/1531432.stm).

Chibots. "Contests." Retrieved February 5, 2010. (http://www.chibots.org).

International Robot Olympiad Committee. "International Robot Olympiad." Retrieved March 30, 2010 (http://www.iroc.org).

KISS Institute for Practical Robotics. "Botball." Retrieved March 20, 2010 (http://www.botball.org/about).

NASA: The Robotics Alliance Project. "Robotic Competitions." Retrieved February 14, 2010 (http://robotics.nasa.gov/events/competitions.php).

Penfield-Harris FIRST Robotics Team. "Team 1511: Rolling Thunder." Retrieved March 15, 2010 (http://www.penfieldrobotics.com).

Randolph, Ryan. *Robotics.* New York, NY: Rosen Publishing Group, 2009.

RoboCup Federation. "RoboCup." Retrieved March 2, 2010 (http://www.robocup.org).

RoboRealm. "Robotic Clubs." Retrieved February 2, 2010 (http://www.roborealm.com/clubs/list.php).

Society of Robots. "Beginners: How to Build Your First Robot Tutorial." Retrieved March 5, 2010 (http://www.societyofrobots.com/robot_tutorial.shtml).

Strickland, Jonathan. "How Nanorobots Will Work." HowStuffWorks. Retrieved April 2, 2010 (http://electronics.howstuffworks.com/nanorobot6.htm).

INDEX

ABOUT THE AUTHOR

Therese Shea is the editor and author of more than one hundred educational nonfiction books. Many focus on advances in science, such as in the field of robotics. A graduate of Providence College, Shea holds an M.A. in English education from the State University of New York at Buffalo. She lives in Buffalo, New York, with her husband, Mark.

PHOTO CREDITS

Cover, pp. 26, 37 Adriana M. Groisman, courtesy of First ®; cover (background), book art Axel Lauerer/ Flickr/Getty Images; pp. 5, 18, 34 Beach Cities Robotics; pp. 7, 22, 24 Chelle Hambric, ILITE Robotics; p. 10 Cameron Spencer/Getty Images; p. 11 Astrid Riecken/ The Washington Times/Landov; p. 13 Wissahickon High School; p. 27 © Zhang Qingyun/Imaginechina/ Zuma; p. 32 Kiss Institute for Practical Robotics © Botball Educational Robotics Program ©; p. 35 photo by New York Yankees and permission from Morris High School Robotics Team.

Designer: Matthew Cauli; Editor: Nicholas Croce; Photo Researcher: Marty Levick